We Vote

Contents

Cynthia Martin

How Children Vote

These children are going to **vote**. They are going to vote on where the class should go on their field trip. Each child in the class will vote for one place. Each child's vote will be counted.

Our Field Trip		
Zoo		ⅢⅡ
Children's Museum		IIII
Aquarium		ⅢⅡ III

This chart shows how the children voted. Votes were counted by making **tally marks**. Each child voted for one place. Each vote got a mark like this: I.

This shows four votes: IIII. This shows five votes: ⅢⅡ.

Most of the **voters** chose the aquarium.

How Adults Vote

Adults vote too. Sometimes people vote by marking a paper called a **ballot**. Then the votes on all the ballots are counted.

Sometimes people vote at a **voting machine**. They vote by moving a handle. The machine counts everyone's votes.

People vote for many reasons. Voting is a way people make choices.

Voting About Safety

In one town, people wanted a good way to keep children safe as they crossed the street. Should there be a crossing guard?

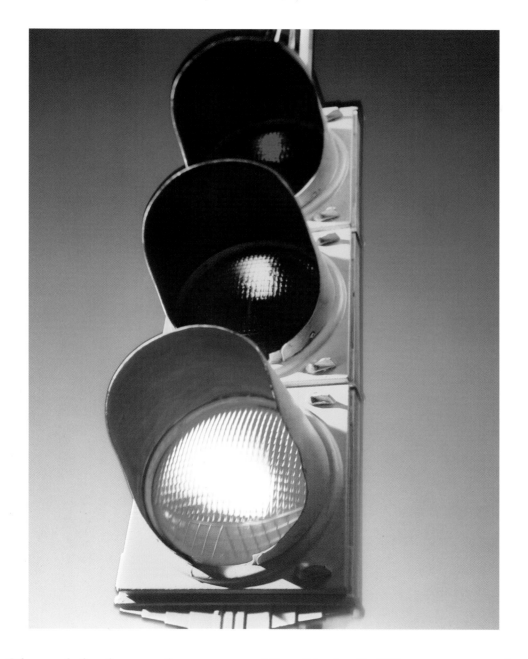

Should there be a traffic light? They voted
for a crossing guard. How would you vote?

Voting About Money

In one town, people voted about how
to spend their town's money. They
had to vote whether to build a library
or a theater.

They did not have enough money for both. They had to decide which was better for their town. How would you vote?

Voting About Space

In another town, people had to vote whether to have a town garden or a town playground. There was space for one. Some people voted for a garden. They thought that families would like to plant vegetables and flowers.

Some people voted for a playground.
They thought that families would like
to have a safe place for children to play.
How would you vote?

People may decide about whether or not to build a mall. In one **community,** people wanted a mall. They voted YES.

In another community, people did not want to have a mall. They voted NO.

Voting for Leaders

In our country, we choose people to be our **leaders**. These pins show pictures of people who wanted to be **president** or **vice president** of our country.

We vote for many reasons. Voting helps us make important choices.

Glossary

ballot: a piece of paper that shows a secret vote

community: a group of people living and working together in the same place

leaders: people who represent larger groups of people in communities

president: the person at the head of a group, community, or country

tally marks: lines used to record and count the number of things in a group

vice president: the person who is next in command after a president

vote: a way a person can show his or her choice

voters: people who vote

voting machine: a machine that counts votes